"Quote...
Unquote"

Nigel Rees

**Illustrated
by
Michael ffolkes**

London
GEORGE ALLEN & UNWIN
Boston   Sydney

First published in 1978
Fourth impression 1979

GEORGE ALLEN & UNWIN LTD
40 Museum Street, London WC1A 1LU

This edition © Nigel Rees 1978
ISBN 0 04 827017 2

Illustrations © Michael ffolkes 1978

British Library Cataloguing in Publication Data

Rees, Nigel
    'Quote–unquote'.
    1. Quotations, English
    I. Title
    808.88'2   PN6081   78–40335

    ISBN 0–04–827017–2

Designed by David Pocknell

Typeset in 10 point Monophoto Plantin Light
and printed and bound in Great Britain
by Biddles Ltd., Guildford and King's Lynn

Contents

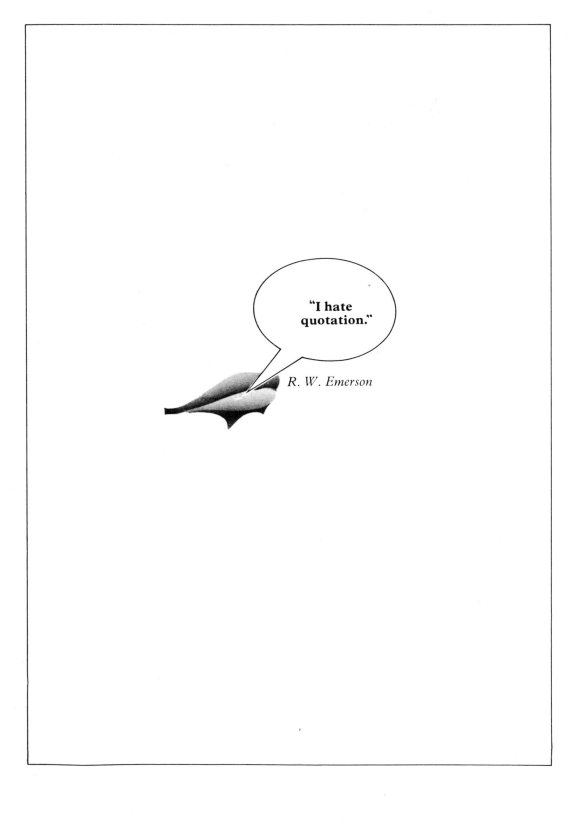

Preface

This is partly a quiz-book and partly an anthology based on the BBC Radio 4 series **'Quote . . . Unquote'**.

I am inclined to interpret the word 'quote' very broadly – so you will find in these pages:

aphorisms, apothegms, asides, banalities, barbs, bons mots, bromides, catchphrases, citations, clichés, commonplaces, cutting remarks, dictums, epigrams, epitaphs, mottoes, put downs, quips, quotes, references, replications, responsions, repartees, retorts, replies, rebuttals, rejoinders, ripostes, sage reflections, sayings, slogans, squelches, unquotes, unsolicited testimonials, wise saws . . . and modern instances.

In devising the radio quiz – and now this book – I have not been restricted by considerations of comprehensiveness, durability or even usefulness, as the compiler of a dictionary of quotations might be.

The **'Quote . . . Unquote'** book simply contains what I have most enjoyed reading or hearing over the past few years and have thought worth jotting down. I hope the overall effect for the reader will be like opening another man's commonplace book.

I should make plain that some of the quotes are bogus. These are what I call the 'unquotes' – inventions perfectly obvious as such, I hope. Should one ever appear in a dictionary of quotations I shall have to award a prize to the person who spots it.

My thanks are due to the BBC for putting the programme on the air, to my estimable producer John Lloyd for working on the idea with me since the very beginning, and to numerous listeners and friends for sharing with me their favourite quotations and pointing out mistakes (I look forward to being told of the ones in this book.)

Those who took part in the quiz during the first two years were, not only brave enough to have their knowledge of quotations exposed, they also provided much ancillary wit – some of which has found its way into this volume:

Larry Adler, Lynn Barber, Richard Boston, James Cameron, Peter Cook, Jilly Cooper, Alan Coren, Ronald Fletcher, Anna Ford, Michael Frayn, Graeme Garden, Benny Green, Germaine Greer, Irene Handl, Richard Ingrams, Jo Kendall, Roberta Leigh, Humphrey Lyttelton, Lord Mancroft, Arthur Marshall, George Melly, Jonathan Miller, Spike Milligan, Malcolm Muggeridge, Ian McKellen, Hilary Pritchard, Diana Quick, Norma Shepherd, Ned Sherrin, Miriam Stoppard, Tom Stoppard, Polly Toynbee, John Wells, Kenneth Williams, Terry Wogan.

'They were all of them fond of quotations.'
(Lewis Carroll, *The Hunting of the Snark*)

Dr Livingstone, I Presume?

These notable first words were spoken by Henry Morton Stanley when at last he located the Scottish missionary and explorer near Lake Tanganyika in 1871.
Here are some more. Who said them? In what sense are they first words?

The answers are over the page.

1

Mr Watson, come here, I want to see you.

2

We knocked the bastard off.

3

That's one small step for man, one giant leap for mankind.

4

Tennis anyone?

5

You ain't heard nothin' yet.

6

God be glorified.

7

The past is a foreign country: they do things differently there.

8

As I was saying when I was interrupted, it is a powerful hard thing to please all the people all the time.

Answers
Dr Livingstone, I Presume?

1

The first words spoken over the telephone by its inventor, Alexander Graham Bell, March 1876.

2

Edmund Hillary on being the first to reach the summit of Mount Everest, May 1953. cf. George Leigh Mallory's reply when asked why he wanted to do the same: 'Because it's there.'

3

The first words spoken on the moon by Neil Armstrong, July 1969.

4

Humphrey Bogart's sole line in his first stage appearance.

5

Ad lib remark by Al Jolson in *The Jazz Singer*, the first full-length talking picture, released in New York, October 1927.

6

Reputed to be the first words of St Nicholas as he leapt from his mother's womb – as in Benjamin Britten's cantata *St Nicholas*.

7

The opening words of L. P. Hartley's novel *The Go-Between*.

8

William Connor, 'Cassandra' of the *Daily Mirror*, resuming his column after the war, September 1946.

Oh, Bitchery

'You should learn not to make personal remarks,' said
Alice to the Mad Hatter – but it did not stop him and it
has not stopped anyone else from doing so.
Here is a selection of my favourite personal
remarks, ranging from the mildly censorious to the
ambiguously flattering:

He didn't need to take a change of shoes. He can
always wear hers. She has very big feet, you know.

> *Vivien Merchant, Harold Pinter's*
> *wife, when he left her for Lady*
> *Antonia Fraser.*

He rose without trace.

> *Kitty Muggeridge on David Frost.*

He is a self-made man and worships his creator.

> *John Bright on Disraeli.*

No more coals to Newcastle, no more Hoares to
Paris.

> *King George V made this remark
> when Sir Samuel Hoare, the Foreign
> Secretary, concluded the Hoare-
> Laval pact (which virtually con-
> signed Abyssinia to the Italians) in
> Paris.*

Winston has devoted the best years of his life to
preparing his impromptu speeches.

> *F. E. Smith.*

The only thing I really mind about going to prison
is the thought of Lord Longford coming to visit me.

> *Richard Ingrams, editor of* Private
> Eye.

Dame Edith Evans was told that Nancy Mitford had been lent a
villa so that she could finish a book:
'Oh really. What exactly is she reading?'

Too clever by three-quarters.

> *said of Jonathan Miller.*

Reminds me of nothing so much as a dead fish
before it has had time to stiffen.

> *George Orwell's remark about
> Clement Attlee typifies the in-
> ordinate amount of personal abuse
> Attlee had levelled at him. Churchill
> is said to have called him 'a sheep in
> sheep's clothing' and 'a modest little
> man with much to be modest about.'
> A popular saying was, 'An empty
> taxi drew up and out got Clem
> Attlee.'*

A legend in his own lunchtime.

> *Christopher Wordsworth, literary*
> *critic, on Clifford Makins, sporting*
> *journalist.*

That woman speaks eighteen languages, and she
can't say 'no' in any of them.

> *Dorothy Parker.*

He looks like the guy in a science fiction movie who
is the first to see the Creature.

*David Frye's description of President
Gerald R. Ford is one of many.*

Others are:

He played too much football without a helmet.

He can't eat gum and walk at the same time.

He'd fuck up a two-car funeral.

In defeat unbeatable, in victory unbearable.

Churchill on Montgomery.

She could eat an apple through a tennis racquet.

*Said of a toothy character in Noel
Coward's* Come into the Garden,
Maud.

Two of the nicest people if ever there was one.

*Alan Bennett on Sidney and
Beatrice Webb.*

**Randolph Churchill went into hospital to have a lung removed
and it was announced that the trouble was not malignant.
Evelyn Waugh commented:**

**'A typical triumph of modern science to find the only part of
Randolph that was not malignant and remove it.'**

What the proprietorship of these papers is aiming at
is power, and power without responsibility, the
privilege of the harlot throughout the ages.

*Harold Macmillan was present at the
by-election meeting in 1931 when
Baldwin made this attack on the
Press Barons. He recalls his father-
in-law, the Duke of Devonshire,
commenting: 'Good God, that's done
it. He's lost us the tarts' vote.'*

The 'T' Is Silent

In any digest of personal remarks Margot Asquith,
wife of the Liberal Prime Minister,
deserves a section to herself.
Sometimes she dropped bricks and was downright insulting,
on other occasions she produced wonderful *margots*,
vivid verbal snapshots like these:

He could not see a belt without hitting below it.

of Lloyd George.

My dear old friend King George V always told me
that he would never have died but for that vile
doctor.

of Lord Dawson of Penn.

His modesty amounts to deformity.

of her husband.

She tells enough white lies to ice a cake.

of a female acquaintance.

He has a brilliant mind until he makes it up.

of Sir Stafford Cripps.

I saw him riding in the Row, clinging to his horse
like a string of onions.

of Lord Hugh Cecil.

An imitation rough diamond.

of a US General.

She's as tough as an ox. She'll be turned into Bovril
when she dies.

of a friend.

Very clever, but his brains go to his head.

of F. E. Smith.

He had one arm round your waist and one eye on the clock.

of a politician.

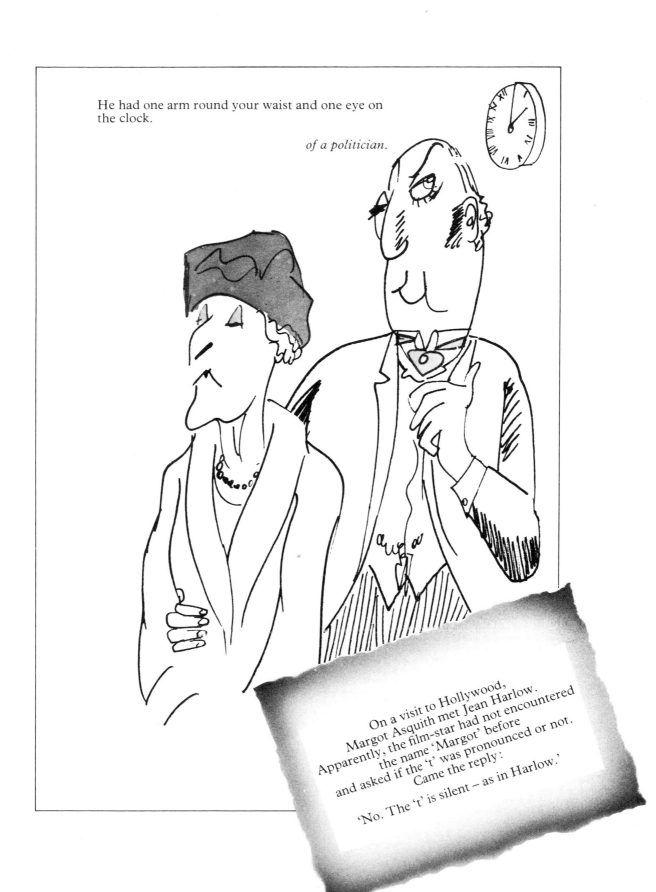

On a visit to Hollywood, Margot Asquith met Jean Harlow. Apparently, the film-star had not encountered the name 'Margot' before and asked if the 't' was pronounced or not. Came the reply:

'No. The 't' is silent – as in Harlow.'

'Old men forget'

Kinquering Congs Their Titles Take – 1

Pity poor Peter Scott, the naturalist, when he came to choose the title
for his autobiography. He set his heart on *The Eye of the Wind*
but nowhere could he find a poem or piece of suitable prose
containing the phrase.
Eventually, in desperation, he asked C. Day Lewis to
write a poem from which he could quote it.
The following writers of bibliography or autobiography did
not have to go to such desperate lengths for their titles.

Where did they go?
The answers are on page 20

1
Hugh Cudlipp: **Publish and be Damned.**

2
Sir Francis Chichester: **The Lonely Sea and the Sky.**

3
Dennis Wheatley: **The Time has come the Young
Man said.**

4
Lilli Palmer: **Change Lobsters and Dance.**

5
T. E. Lawrence: **Seven Pillars of Wisdom.**

6
Richard Hillary: **The Last Enemy.**

7
Duff Cooper: **Old Men Forget.**

8
The Duchess of Windsor: **The Heart has its
Reasons.**

9

Hugh Dalton: **Call Back Yesterday.**

10

Lord George-Brown: **In My Way.**

Where did these writers and composers of plays and musicals find their titles?

11

Thornton Wilder: **The Skin of our Teeth.**

12

George Bernard Shaw: **Arms and the Man.**

13

J. M. Barrie: **Dear Brutus.**

14

Noel Coward: **Sigh No More.**

15

Noel Coward: **This Happy Breed.**

16

Noel Coward: **Blithe Spirit.**

17

Ivor Novello: **Perchance to Dream.**

18

Dorothy Reynolds and Julian Slade: **Salad Days.**

19

Kenneth Tynan and Co.: **Oh, Calcutta.**

'Arms and the man'

GALATEA

Answers

Kinquering Congs Their Titles Take – 1

1 The Duke of Wellington's response when a former mistress threatened to publish her diary and letters.

2 John Masefield's poem *Sea Fever*.

3 ' "The time has come," the Walrus said, / "To talk of many things" ' (Carroll, *Through the Looking-Glass*) coupled with ' "You are old, Father William," the Young Man said' (Carroll, *Alice's Adventures in Wonderland*).

4 Also a reference to *Alice's Adventures in Wonderland*, though these precise words do not appear in 'The Lobster Quadrille'.

5 'Wisdom hath builded her house, she hath hewn out her seven pillars' – Proverbs ix.1.

6 'The last enemy that shall be destroyed is death' – 1 Corinthians xv.26.

7 'Old men forget . . . / But he'll remember with advantages / What feats he did that day [St Crispin's Day]' – Shakespeare, *Henry V*, IV.iii.

8 'Le cœur a ses raisons que la raison ne connaît point' – Pascal, *Pensées*.

9 'O! call back yesterday, bid time return' – Shakespeare, *Richard II*, III.ii.

10 Lord George-Brown attributes it to 'My Way' though the song does not include this phrase.

11 'I am escaped with the skin of my teeth' – Job xix.20.

12 'Arma virumque cano' – the opening words of Virgil's *Aeneid*, or from Dryden's translation: 'Arms, and the man I sing.'

13 'The fault, dear Brutus, is not in our stars' – Shakespeare, *Julius Caesar*, I.ii.

14 'Sigh no more, ladies, sigh no more / Men were deceivers ever' – Shakespeare, *Much Ado about Nothing*, I.iii.

15 'This Royal throne of kings, this sceptr'd isle / . . . this happy breed of men' – Shakespeare, *Richard II*, II.i.

16 'Hail to thee, blithe spirit, bird thou never wert' – Shelley, 'To a Skylark'.

17 'To die, to sleep: / To sleep, perchance to dream' – Shakespeare, *Hamlet*, III.i.

18 'My salad days, when I was green in judgement, cold in blood' – Shakespeare, *Antony and Cleopatra*, I.v.

19 'Oh, quel cul t'as' – 'Oh, what a lovely bum you have.'

'Oh, Calcutta...'

Like The Curate's Egg – 1

The Du Maurier cartoon 'True Humility' appeared in *Punch* on 19 November 1895. It showed a bishop at breakfast with a curate, and the caption read:

Rt Rev. Host
I'm afraid you've got a bad egg, Mr Jones.
The Curate
Oh no, my Lord, I assure you! Parts of it are excellent.

Like the Curate's egg, the following quotations are good in parts, but parts of them are scrambled. What was the original quotation? What is the source?

The answers are on page 24.

1

A rose-red city, half as Golders Green.

2

There is a tide in the affairs of women which, taken at the flood, leads – God knows where.

3
Vasectomy means not ever having to say you're sorry.

4
Brevity is the soul of lingerie.

5

'Tis better to have loved and lost than never to have
lost at all.

6

Man is born free but everywhere is in cellular
underwear.

7

Kinquering congs their titles take.

8

Where there is no television, the people perish.

9

Live music is an anachronism, and now is the winter of
our discothèque.

10

I awoke one morning and found myself famished.

11

Oh, wad some power the giftie gie us to see some
people before they see us.

12

Ralph Reader, I married him.

13

When I am dead and opened, you shall find 'Callous'
engraved upon my heart.

14

Great oafs from little infants grow.

Answers
Like The Curate's Egg – 1

1 'A rose-red city – "half as old as time"'! – Rev. John William Burgon, *Petra*. The quote-within-a-quote refers to 'By many a temple half as old as time', from *Italy: a farewell* by Samuel Rogers. (Scrambled by Muir and Norden in their sketch *Balham: Gateway to the South*, performed on record by Peter Sellers.)

2 'There is a tide in the affairs of men,/Which, taken at the flood, leads on to fortune' – Shakespeare, *Julius Caesar*, IV.iii. (Scrambled by Byron in *Don Juan*.)

3 'Love means not ever having to say you're sorry' – Erich Segal, *Love Story*. (Scrambled by Larry Adler who once took part in an edition of *Quote . . . Unquote* on his way to have a vasectomy.)

4 'Brevity is the soul of wit' – the proverb, which makes its first recorded appearance in Shakespeare's *Hamlet*, II.ii. (Scrambled by Dorothy Parker.)

5 ''Tis better to have loved and lost / Than never to have loved at all' – Tennyson, *In Memoriam*. (Scrambled by Samuel Butler in *Erewhon*.)

6 'Man was born free and everywhere he is in chains' – Jean-Jacques Rousseau, *Du Contrat Social*. (Scrambled by Jonathan Miller in *Beyond the Fringe*.)

7 'Conquering Kings their titles take' – from the hymn by John Chandler. (Scrambled by Rev. W. A. Spooner, supposedly when announcing the hymn in New College chapel, Oxford. As it was not the custom to announce hymns in his day this is one of many 'spoonerisms' of doubtful authenticity.)

8 'Where there is no vision, the people perish' – Proverbs xxix.18.

9 'Now is the winter of our discontent' – Shakespeare, *Richard III*, I.i. (Scrambled by Benny Green in a newspaper article.)

10 'I awoke one morning and found myself famous' – Byron on the instantaneous success of *Childe Harold*.

11 'O wad some Pow'r the giftie gie us / To see oursels as others see us' – Robert Burns, *To a louse*. (Scrambled by Ethel Watts Mumford.)

12 'Reader, I married him' – the opening words of the last chapter of *Jane Eyre* by Charlotte Bronte, referring to Mr Rochester rather than the founder of the Boy Scout *Gang Show*.

13 'When I am dead and opened you shall find "Calais" lying in my heart' – the saying attributed to Mary Tudor, Calais having been lost to the French after two hundred years as an English possession. (Scrambled by Sellars and Yeatman in *1066 and all that*.)

14 'Great oaks from little acorns grow' – the proverb. (Scrambled by various people. Another version, concerning Nikita Kruschev, is 'Great oafs from little ikons grow.')

MENU

Cheer Up, The *Wurst* Is Yet To Come

'I eat like a vulture,' said Groucho. 'Unfortunately, the resemblance doesn't end there . . .'

The **Quote . . . Table d'hôte** is a menu made up of misprints and mistranslations observed in restaurants as far afield as Rome, Paris, Barcelona and the Caledonian Road.

Half fresh grapefruit
Satiated calamary
Hen soup
Hard egg with sauce mayonnaise
Frightened eggs

Dreaded veal cutlet
Larks in the spit
Spited rooster
Battered codpieces
A kind of long
Utmost of chicken
Veal Gordon Blue
Raped carrots

Sweet smalls pie★
Tarts of the house at pleasure

Café au lit

★ 'Age cannot wither it, nor custard stale its infinite variety' Shakespeare, *Antony and Cleopatra* I.ii.

To wash it all down – or away – may we recommend, as did a wine importer, the Nuits St Georges '64:

Deep colour and big, shaggy nose. Rather a jumbly, untidy sort of wine, with fruitiness shooting off one way, firmness another, and body pushing about underneath. It will be as comfortable and comforting as the 1961 Nuits St Georges when it has pulled its ends in and settled down.

To round off the meal, a drop of port perhaps? Lord Mancroft remembers how Stephen Potter, inventor of One-Upmanship, once promoted a Cockburn '97 which was clearly past its best. He spoke of:

the imperial decay of the invalid port . . . its gracious withdrawal from perfection . . . keeping a hint of former majesty, withal . . . whilst it hovered between oblivion and the divine *Untergang* of infinite recession.

Replies Retorts Ripostes

Lord Nuffield, the motor magnate, had dined at an Oxford college. A porter produced his hat rather briskly and Nuffield inquired, 'How d'you know it's mine?' The porter replied:

> *I don't, my Lord. But it's the one you came with.*

Martin Routh (1755–1854) was President of Magdalen College, Oxford, and a man of great composure – so much so that when an excitable Fellow rushed up to announce that a member of the college had killed himself, Routh replied:

> *Pray, don't tell me who. Allow me to guess.*

Sir Thomas Beecham was travelling in the no-smoking carriage of a train when a woman passenger lit a cigarette with the words, 'You won't object if I smoke?' To which Beecham replied, 'Certainly not – and you won't object if I'm sick.'
It was in the days when the railways were still privately owned. 'I don't think you know who I am,' the woman angrily pointed out. 'I am one of the directors' wives.'
To which Beecham riposted:

> *Madam, if you were the director's only wife, I should still be sick.*

When Samuel Goldwyn asked Bernard Shaw if he could buy the film rights to his plays, G.B.S. declined the offer thus:

> *The trouble is, Mr Goldwyn, that you are only interested in art and I am only interested in money.*

Horatio Bottomley, the Independent MP sent to gaol for fraudulent conversion in 1922, was discovered sewing mail-bags by a prison visitor. 'Ah, Bottomley,' he remarked. 'Sewing?'

> *No, reaping.*

'Pearls before swine'

Calvin Coolidge once made a notable squelch. A young girl gushed: 'Oh, Mr President, Poppa says that if I can get three words out of you he will buy me a fur coat.'

> *Poppa wins.*

Dorothy Parker, when told that Coolidge was dead, remarked:

> *How can they tell?*

And, although said to be apocryphal, there is the story of Dorothy Parker going through a swing-door with Clare Booth Luce who said – as one does on such occasions – 'Age before beauty.' Going ahead first, Parker said:

> *Pearls before swine.*

Eva Perón once visited Europe but was not received as she thought appropriate for the powerful wife of the ruler of Argentina. She failed to get an invitation to tea at Buckingham Palace or the Papal honour she hoped for in Rome. And in northern Italy she complained to her host that a voice in a crowd had called her a 'whore'. He replied:

> *Quite so. But I have not been on a ship for fifteen years and they still call me 'Admiral'.*

It was suggested to Tennyson that the marriage of Thomas and Jane Carlyle was a mistake. With anyone but each other they might have been perfectly happy:

> *I totally disagree with you. By any other arrangement* four *people would have been unhappy instead of* two.

Mandy Rice-Davies, one of the call-girls in the Profumo Affair, 1963, appeared at a magistrates' hearing. She was asked if she was aware that the then Lord Astor had denied her statement that she had been to bed with him:

> *Well, he would, wouldn't he?*

F. E. Smith, Earl of Birkenhead, taunted Lord
Chief Justice Hewart about the size of his stomach.
'What's it to be – a boy or a girl?'

> *If it's a boy I'll call him John. If it's*
> *a girl I'll call her Mary. But if, as I*
> *suspect, it's only wind, I'll call it*
> *F. E. Smith.*

The Irish actor-manager Anew McMaster was
travelling with his company by train one Sunday
when it stopped at an isolated rural station.
Lowering the window and revealing his extravagant
hat and other thespian garb, McMaster inquired of
a porter, 'What country, friend, is this?' Being an
educated Irish railway employee, the porter recognised Viola's opening lines from *Twelfth Night*
and promptly gave Shakespeare's own reply:

> *This is Illyria – lady.*

Jack Benny, to the robber who demanded 'Your
money or your life!':

> *I'm thinking it over.*

W. C. Fields, when asked whether he liked
children:

> *Boiled or fried?*

Shaw sent Churchill two tickets for the first night of
St Joan, 'one for yourself, one for a friend – if you
have one'. Expressing regret at not being able to
attend, Churchill replied by requesting tickets for
the second night:

If there is one.

Towards the end of his life, Churchill was sitting in
the House of Commons smoking room with his fly-
buttons undone. When this was pointed out to him,
he said:

Dead birds don't fall out of nests.

A business-like exchange of notes in the eighteenth
century between the Prince de Joinville and the
actress, Mlle Rachel. He asked, 'Where? When?
How much?' She answered:

Your place. Tonight. Free.

Groucho Marx was going down in the lift at the
Hotel Danieli in Venice. At the fourth floor a group
of priests got in. One of them recognised Groucho
and said, 'Excuse me, Mr Marx, but my mother was
a great fan of yours.' To which Groucho retorted:

*I didn't know you guys were allowed
to have mothers.*

The wife of Chico Marx caught him kissing a
chorus-girl. A row ensued, tempers flared, but the
only explanation Chico offered was:

*I wasn't kissing her. I was whispering
in her mouth.*

When Ringo Starr was asked what was the greatest
threat to the Beatles – the H-Bomb or dandruff, he
answered:

*The H-Bomb. We've already got
dandruff.*

A fan accosted James Joyce in Zurich with the
words 'May I kiss the hand that wrote *Ulysses*?'
Joyce refused saying:

No, it did a lot of other things, too.

In the First World War, Lytton Strachey appeared before a military tribunal to put his case as a conscientious objector. He was asked by the chairman what he would do if he saw a German soldier trying to rape his sister:

I would try to get between them.

When Noel Coward was confronted by middle-aged female fans who began, 'Oh, Mr Coward, you don't know me . . .', he would say:

But, of course, I do. And how is Mabel?

Coward watched the Coronation on TV in New York. When the carriage bearing Queen Salote of Tonga came into view a friend asked, 'Who's the fellow sitting with her?' In fact, it was the Sultan of Kelantan but Coward suggested:

Her lunch.

There's No Answer To That

Frank Finlay (as Casanova)
I'll be perfectly frank with you – I have a long felt want.
Eric Morecambe
There's no answer to that.

Here are some more remarks to which a reply is
neither recorded nor, in most cases, conceivable:

Which of us has not felt in his heart a half-warmed
fish?

> *Rev. W. A. Spooner.*

Tell me, was it you or your brother who was killed
in the war?

> *Spooner, again.*

Anyone who isn't confused here doesn't really
understand what's going on.

> *Belfast citizen, 1970.*

Ah well, they say it's not as bad as they say it is.

> *Southern Irish woman on the
> situation in Ulster.*

A great man! Why, I doubt if there are six his equal
in the whole of Boston.

> *Unnamed Bostonian to Gladstone
> about Shakespeare.*

The most delightful advantage of being bald – one
can *hear* snowflakes.

> *R. G. Daniels.*

Ernie Byfield Jnr, son of the American hotel owner,
was asked why he – such a young man – was run-
ning three big hotels:

> *Well, I happened to run into my
> father in the lobby and he took a
> liking to me.*

Oh no, thank you, I only smoke on special
occasions.

> *Labour minister when asked if he
> would like a cigar, while dining with
> King George VI.*

The down trains will be delayed owing to the late
arrival of the up trains.

> *Station announcer at Waterloo.*

Welsh miner, when asked if he was ready to strike,
in 1973:

> *We have girded up our loins and tied
> up the loose ends.*

A woman without a man is like a fish without a
bicycle.

> *Graffito at Birmingham University
> (and elsewhere).*

I wouldn't believe Hitler was dead, even if he told
me so himself.

> *Hjalmar Schacht, Hitler's Central
> Bank Governor, 8 May 1945.*

Why did He not marry? Could the answer be that
Jesus was not by nature the marrying sort?

> *Hugh Montefiore, when Vicar of St
> Mary's, Cambridge.*

I used to be indecisive, but now I'm not so sure.

> *Boscoe Pertwee (eighteenth-century
> wit).*

The soil is fertile, sir, because it is full of micro-
orgasms.

> *Thirteen-year-old pupil at
> Cranleigh.*

When Sir John Gielgud told a theatrical company
that all the men must wear jock-straps under their
leotards, a voice piped up:

> *Please, Sir John, does that apply to
> those of us who only have small
> parts?*

I think that the gentleman who created 'King Kong'
would have been more gainfully employed in
making a set of concrete steps at the Ashton Road
end of Bracebridge Street to help old people get to
the bus without having to make half-mile detours.

> *Letter to the* Birmingham Evening
> Mail, *May 1972.*

Is it a book that you would have lying around in
your own house? Is this a book that you would even
wish your wife or your servant to read?

> *Mervyn Griffith-Jones, prosecuting
> counsel at the* Lady Chatterley *trial,
> 1961.*

The weather will be cold. There are two reasons for
this. One is that the temperatures will be lower.

> *Radio weather forecast, 12 April,
> 1969.*

You should make a point of trying every experience
once – except incest and folk dancing.

> *Scotsman (quoted by Arnold Bax).*

Quote . . . Misquote

Misquotation is not necessarily a vice. We tend to rearrange words to make them easier to utter. We may attribute words to a speaker which he did not actually say but which convey the spirit of what he said. In what way are these misquotes? What was originally said or meant?

The answers are on page 40.

1

I knew him well, Horatio.

2

Play it again, Sam.

3

Thou shalt not kill / But needst not strive officiously to keep alive.

4

We are the masters now.

5

All that glitters is not gold.

6

Come up and see me some time.

7

Money is the root of all evil.

8

Survival of the fittest.

9

Lead on, Macduff.

10

I want to be alone.

11

Pride goeth before a fall.

12

The stuff that dreams are made of.

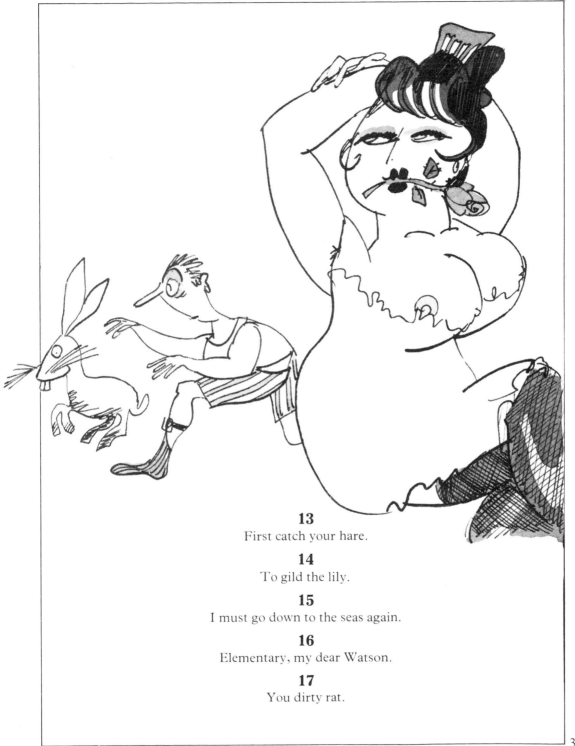

13

First catch your hare.

14

To gild the lily.

15

I must go down to the seas again.

16

Elementary, my dear Watson.

17

You dirty rat.

Answers
Quote . . . Misquote

1

Hamlet's actual words are: 'Alas! poor Yorick. I knew him, Horatio.' (*Hamlet*, V.i)

2

Nowhere in the film *Casablanca* does Humphrey Bogart say this phrase. At one point Ingrid Bergman says, 'Play it once, Sam, for old time's sake' and later on Bogart says, 'You played it for her, you can play it for me. Play it.'

3

Arthur Hugh Clough's *The Latest Decalogue* was an *ironical* version of the Ten Commandments – not serious advice to doctors (in which sense it is often quoted now).

4

What Sir Hartley Shawcross said in the House of Commons in April 1946 was: 'We [Labour] are the masters *at the moment* – and not only for the moment but for a very long time to come.'

5

If quoting from *The Merchant of Venice* (II.vii): 'All that *glisters* is not gold.'

6

Nowhere in the film *She done him wrong* does Mae West say the words in that order. She says: 'You know I always did like a man in uniform. And that one fits you grand. Why don't you *come up some time and see me.*'

7

'*The love of money* is the root of all evil' – 1 Timothy vi.10.

8

Herbert Spencer meant the survival of the most suitable, not of the most fit physically.

9

'*Lay on*, Macduff. / And damn'd be him that first cries, "Hold enough!"' – *Macbeth*, V.vii.

10

'I never said I want to be alone,' Garbo once re-marked. 'I only said I want to be *let* alone.' Indeed, no one has been able to find mention of the famous phrase in any newspaper reports of her early days in Hollywood. After it had caught on, however, she herself used it in various films.

11

'*Pride goeth before destruction* and an haughty spirit before a fall' – Proverbs xvi.18.

12

'We are such stuff / As dreams are made *on*' – *The Tempest*.

13

A misquote and usually misattributed, too. Not Mrs Beeton but Mrs Hannah Glasse wrote 'Take your hare when it is cased' in *The Art of Cookery made plain and easy*, 1747.

14

In quoting *King John* (IV.ii): '*To gild refined gold*, to paint the lily.'

15

'I must down to the seas again' – Masefield, *Sea Fever*.

16

The nearest the great detective gets to saying this occurs in *The Memoirs of Sherlock Holmes* when he remarks to Watson: 'Elementary.'

17

James Cagney claims he never said the words put in his mouth by numerous impressionists. In *Blonde Crazy*, however, he calls someone a 'dirty, double-crossing rat'.

A Week Is A Long Time in Politics

Uncharacteristically, Sir Harold Wilson says he is unable to remember when he first uttered what is without doubt the most quoted political remark of recent years – 'A week is a long time in politics'.

What is more, he says 'it does not mean I'm living from day to day', but was intended as 'a prescription for long-term strategic thinking and planning, ignoring the day-to-day issues and pressures which may hit the headlines but which must not be allowed to get out of focus while longer-term policies are taking effect'.

It seems most probable that in its present form the phrase was first uttered at a meeting of the Parliamentary Lobby in the wake of the Sterling crisis shortly after Harold Wilson came to power in 1964.

However, Robert Carvel of the London *Evening Standard* recalls Wilson at a Labour Party conference in 1960 saying 'Forty-eight hours is a long time in politics'.

Even quotes are prone to inflation.

Here are some more political sayings from the past decade or two. See also the chapters *Expletive Deleted* and *Better Left Unsaid*.

Power is the ultimate aphrodisiac.★

> *Henry Kissinger.*

If the British public falls for Labour's policies, I say it will be stark staring bonkers.

> *Quintin Hogg, before the 1964 general election which brought Labour to power.*

Greater love hath no man than this, that he lay down his friends for his life.

> *Jeremy Thorpe, on Harold Macmillan's 'Night of the Long Knives' when he sacked half his Cabinet, 1962.*

★This should not be confused with Lord Acton's dictum: 'All power tends to be an aphrodisiac and absolute power leaves you feeling rotten by Wednesday'.

As I look ahead I am filled with foreboding. Like
the Roman I seem to see 'The River Tiber foaming
with much blood.'

> *Enoch Powell's audience in
> Birmingham, April 1968, im-
> mediately spotted this as a reference
> to Virgil's* Aeneid, *Book Six: 'Et
> Thybrim multo spumantem sanguine
> cerno.'*

All reactionaries are paper tigers.

> *Mao Tse-Tung.*

Most British statesmen have either drunk too much
or womanised too much. I never fell into the second
category.

> *Lord George-Brown.*

Lord George-Brown drunk is a better man than the
Prime Minister sober.

> *Leader in* The Times.

I thought the best thing to do was to settle up these
little local difficulties and then return to the wider
vision of the Commonwealth.

> *Harold Macmillan said this on
> leaving for the Commonwealth
> Conference in 1958. Peter
> Thorneycroft, his Chancellor of the
> Exchequer, and two Treasury
> ministers had just resigned.*

Every time Mr Macmillan comes back from abroad
Mr Butler goes to the airport and grips him warmly
by the throat.

> *Harold Wilson.*

You won the election. But I won the count.

> *Anastasio Somoza, Nicaraguan
> dictator.*

I think the Prime Minister has to be a butcher and
know the joints. That is perhaps where I have not
been competent enough in knowing the ways that
you cut up a carcass.

> R. A. Butler (cf. Gladstone: 'The
> first essential for a Prime Minister is
> to be a good butcher.')

I am on the right wing of the middle of the road
with a strong radical bias.

> Anthony Wedgwood-Benn in the
> mid-1950s.

It is the unacceptable face of capitalism but one
should not suggest that the whole of British in-
dustry consists of practices of this kind.

> Edward Heath on the Lonrho Affair,
> 1973.

Bunnies *can* (and *will*) go to France.

> Jeremy Thorpe to a Mr Norman
> Scott, 1961.

Ich bin ein Berliner.

> President Kennedy, West Berlin,
> 1963. (According to Ben Bradlee he
> spent 'the better part of an hour'
> learning how to pronounce this
> phrase.)

I would remind you that extremism in the defense
of liberty is no vice and . . . that moderation in the
pursuit of justice is no virtue.

> Senator Barry Goldwater, 1964.

I'm an optimist. But I'm an optimist who takes his
raincoat.

> Harold Wilson.

We have, of course, often done it before, but never on a pavement outside a hotel in Eastbourne. We have done it in various rooms in one way or another at various functions. It is perfectly genuine and normal – and normal and right – so to do.

William Whitelaw on kissing
Margaret Thatcher, 1975.

All political lives, unless they are cut off in mid-stream at a happy juncture, end in failure, because that is the nature of politics and of human affairs.

Enoch Powell.

The Prime Minister is stealing our clothes . . . but he's going to look pretty ridiculous walking around in mine.

Margaret Thatcher, 1977.

Kinquering Congs Their Titles Take – 2

Where did these kinquering novelists take their titles from?

The answers are on page 50

1

William Thackeray: **Vanity Fair.**

2

Frederick Forsyth: **The Dogs of War.**

3

John Steinbeck: **The Grapes of Wrath.**

4

John Steinbeck: **Of Mice and Men.**

5

Ernest Hemingway: **For Whom the Bell Tolls.**

6

Nigel Balchin: **Mine own Executioner.**

7

James Jones: **From here to Eternity.**

8

W. Somerset Maugham: **Cakes and Ale.**

9

Mary Webb: **Precious Bane.**

10

Taylor Caldwell: **Captains and the Kings.**

11

Aldous Huxley: **Antic Hay.**

12

Aldous Huxley: **Brave New World.**

13

Susan Howatch: **The Rich are Different.**

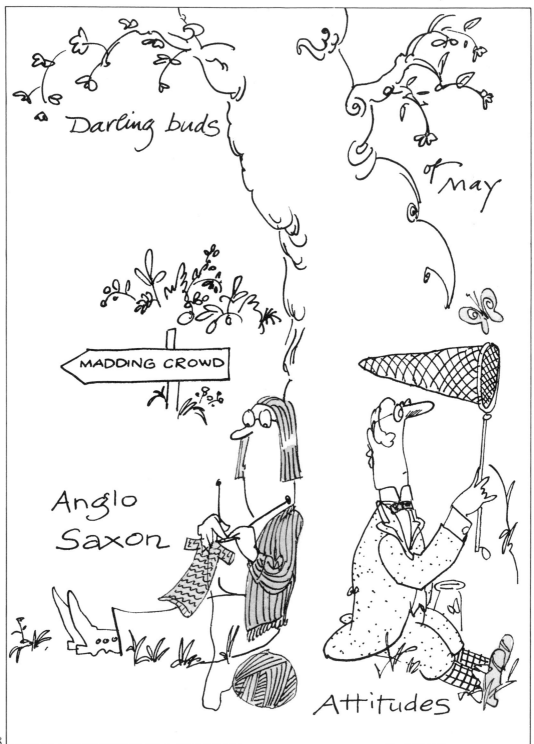

14

Thomas Hardy: **Far from the Madding Crowd.**

15

Thomas Hardy: **Under the Greenwood Tree.**

16

Angus Wilson: **Anglo-Saxon Attitudes.**

17

Simon Raven: the **Alms for Oblivion** series.

18

H. E. Bates: **The Darling Buds of May.**

19

T. H. White: **The Once and Future King.**

20

Malcolm Bradbury: **Eating People is Wrong.**

Answers
Kinquering Congs Their Titles Take – 2

1

'It beareth the name of Vanity-Fair, because the town where 'tis kept, is lighter than vanity' – Bunyan, *Pilgrim's Progress*.

2

'Cry "Havoc!" and let slip the dogs of war' – Shakespeare, *Julius Caesar*, III.i.

3

'Mine eyes have seen the glory of the coming of the Lord: / He is trampling out the vintage where the grapes of wrath are stored' – Julia Ward Howe, *The Battle Hymn of the Republic*.

4

'The best laid schemes o' mice an' men / Gang aft a-gley' – Robert Burns, *To a Mouse*.

5

'Any man's death diminishes me, because I am involved in Mankind; And therefore never send to know for whom the bell tolls; It tolls for thee' – John Donne, *Devotions*.

6

'But I do nothing upon my self, and yet I am mine own Executioner' – John Donne, *Devotions* (again).

7

'Gentlemen-rankers out on the spree, / Damned from here to Eternity' – Rudyard Kipling, *Gentlemen Rankers*.

8

'Dost thou think, because thou art virtuous, there shall be no more cakes and ale?' – Shakespeare, *Twelfth Night*, II.iii.

9

'Let none admire / That riches grow in hell; that soil may best / Deserve the precious bane' – Milton, *Paradise Lost*.

10

'The tumult and the shouting dies; / The Captains and the Kings depart' – Kipling, *Recessional*.

11

'My men, like satyrs grazing on the lawns, / Shall with their goat-feet dance an antic hay' – Marlowe, *Edward II*.

12

'O brave new world, / That has such people in't' – Shakespeare, *The Tempest*, V.i.

13

F. Scott Fitzgerald: 'The rich are different from us.' Ernest Hemingway: 'Yes, they have more money.'

14

'Far from the madding crowd's ignoble strife' – Gray, *Elegy Written in a Country Churchyard*.

15

'Under the greenwood tree / Who loves to lie with me' – Shakespeare, *As You Like It*, II.v.

16

'He's an Anglo-Saxon Messenger – and those are Anglo-Saxon attitudes' – Carroll, *Through the Looking-Glass*.

17

'Time hath, my lord, a wallet at his back, / Wherein he puts alms for oblivion' – Shakespeare, *Troilus and Cressida*, III.iii.

18

'Rough winds do shake the darling buds of May' – Shakespeare, *Sonnets*, 18.

19

'Hic jacet Arthurus, rex quondam, rexque futurus' – Malory, *Le Morte d'Arthur*.

20

Song, *The Reluctant Cannibal*, by Flanders and Swann.

Let's Fill the Whole Screen With Tits

Hunt Stromberg, the American film producer, was
discussing a documentary about the South Seas. 'Boys,
I've got an idea,' he declared. 'Let's fill the whole
screen with tits.'

Joseph von Sternberg, the director, said of
Hollywood:

*You can seduce a man's wife there,
attack his daughter and wipe your
hands on his canary, but if you don't
like his movie, you're dead.*

Alfred Hitchcock was once reported as saying that
'Actors are like cattle.' But he denied this.

*What I said was 'Actors should be
treated like cattle.'*

When Norma Shearer, the actress, and Irving Thalberg, the producer,
had their first baby, Eddie Cantor sent them a telegram:

CONGRATULATIONS ON YOUR LATEST
PRODUCTION STOP SURE IT WILL LOOK
BETTER AFTER IT HAS BEEN CUT STOP

*Now, try your hand at spotting who said these famous
lines and in which films.*

The answers are on page 54.

1

In a month from now this Hollywood big shot's going
to give you what you want.

Too late. They start shooting in a week.

I'm going to make him an offer he can't refuse.

2

Fasten your seat-belts. It's gonna be a bumpy night.

3

You know what the fellow said . . . in Italy for thirty
years under the Borgias they had warfare, terror,
murder, bloodshed but they produced Michelangelo,
Leonardo da Vinci, and the Renaissance. In
Switzerland, they had brotherly love, they had five
hundred years of democracy and peace. And what did
that produce? The cuckoo-clock.

4

Water? Do I need it. I've had to shoot my horse.

5

You know you don't have to act with me, Steve. You
don't have to say anything, and you don't have to do
anything. Not a thing . . . or maybe just whistle. You
know how to whistle, don't you, Steve? You just put
your lips together and blow.

6

Louis, I think this is the beginning of a beautiful
friendship.

7

Tomorrow is another day.

8

I think it would be fun to run a newspaper.

9

Nobody's perfect!

10

Beulah, peel me a grape.

Answers
Lets Fill The Whole Screen With Tits

1

Marlon Brando, *The Godfather*.

2

Bette Davis, *All About Eve*.

3

Orson Welles, *The Third Man*. (In fact, he added these lines to
the Graham Greene-Carol Reed script.)

4

Clark Gable in a B picture, *The Painted Desert* – his first words on
screen.

5

Lauren Bacall to Humphrey Bogart, *To Have and Have Not*.

6

Humphrey Bogart to Claude Rains, the last words of *Casablanca*.

7

Vivien Leigh, *Gone With the Wind* –last words (also of Margaret
Mitchell's book).

8

The last words of *Citizen Kane*. Kane's last word is, of course,
'Rosebud'.

9

Joe E. Brown to Jack Lemmon, the last words of *Some Like it
Hot*.

10

Mae West, *I'm No Angel*.

'Water? Do I need it. I've had to shoot my horse.'

Samuel Goldfish Productions

When a Pole arrived in the United States bearing an unpro-
nounceable monicker, an immigration official renamed him
'Goldfish'. Eventually he realised the trick that had been played
on him and took the name 'Goldwyn'. But even as a successful
Hollywood producer Samuel Goldwyn never quite managed to
get to grips with the English language, as countless
'Goldwynisms' – apocryphal or not – prove:

Every director bites the hand that lays the golden egg.

Who wants to go out and see a bad movie when they can stay at
home and see a bad one free on TV?

We have all passed a lot of water since then.

A verbal contract isn't worth the paper it's written on.

The reason so many people showed up at Louis B. Meyer's
funeral was because they wanted to make sure he was dead.

Going to call him 'William'? What kind of a name is that? Every
Tom, Dick and Harry's called William. Why don't you call him
'Bill'?

Yes, my wife's hands are very beautiful. I'm going to have a bust
made of them.

Why only *twelve* disciples? Go out and get thousands!

If you can't give me your word of honour, will you give me your
promise?

From the rails of a liner leaving for Europe, to friends on the
quay:
Bon Voyage!

Very Interesting . . . But Stupid

Arte Johnson used to deliver his catchphrase on *Rowan and Martin's Laugh-In* as a German soldier peeping through a fern. The show had a dozen or more catchphrases. *ITMA* had getting on for forty.
Test your knowledge of catchphrases.
The answers are on page 60.

With which entertainers do you associate these:

1

Can you hear me, mother?

2

I'm in charge.

3

Before your very eyes.

4

Right monkey.

5

The day war broke out.

6

I wanna tell you a story.

7

Hello, my darlings.

8

Now here's another fine mess you've gotten us into.

9

Oh, calamity.

10

Just like that.

In which shows were these catchphrases used?

11

Give him the money, Barney.

12

Ee, it was agony, Ivy.

13

Seriously though, he's doing a grand job.

14

I'll give it five.

15

Oh, get in there Moreton.

16

I only asked.

17

Not a word to Bessie.

18

And now for something completely different.

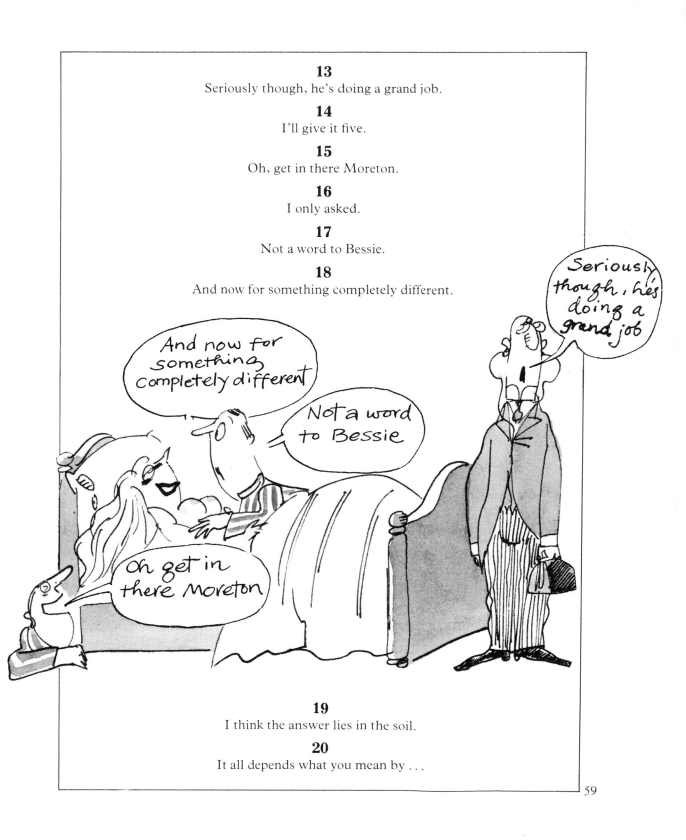

19

I think the answer lies in the soil.

20

It all depends what you mean by . . .

Answers
Very Interesting . . . But Stupid

1

Sandy Powell.

2

Bruce Forsyth.

3

Arthur Askey.

4

Al Read.

5

Robb Wilton.

6

Max Bygraves (he inherited it from people doing
impressions of him . . .).

7

Charlie Drake.

8

Oliver Hardy.

9

Robertson Hare.

10

Tommy Cooper.

11

Have a Go (Wilfred Pickles referring to the producer,
Barney Colehan).

12

Ray's a Laugh (Mrs Hoskin, played by Bob Pearson).

13

That Was The Week That Was (various characters.
Ned Sherrin, the producer, says it was only uttered
half a dozen times).

14

Thank Your Lucky Stars (Janice Nicholls, member of a
pop jury).

15

Educating Archie (Robert Moreton).

16

The Army Game (Bernard Bresslaw).

17

Much Binding in the Marsh (Kenneth Horne).

18

Monty Python's Flying Circus.

19

Beyond our Ken (Kenneth Williams as Arthur
Fallowfield).

20

The Brains Trust (C. E. M. Joad).

Great God! This Is An Awful Place

So said Captain Scott of the South Pole. The following
quotations – complimentary or otherwise – are all about places.
Where do they refer to? Who said them?

The answers are on page 64

1

The shortest way out of _____ is notoriously a bottle of
Gordon's Gin.

2

One has no great hopes from _____. I always say there is
something direful in the sound.

3

Very flat, _____.

4

The Great Wen.

5

If you are lucky enough to have lived in _____ as a young
man, it stays with you; for _____ is a moveable feast.

6

Four thousand holes in _____. And though the holes were
rather small, they had to count them all.

7

_____ is like eating an entire box of chocolate liqueurs at
one go.

8

Home of lost causes, and forsaken beliefs, and unpopular
names, and impossible loyalties!

9

Good Americans when they die go to _____.

10

And when bad Americans die they go to _____.

Answers
Great God This Is An Awful Place

1

Manchester. William Bolitho.

2

Birmingham. Mrs Elton in *Emma* by Jane Austen.

3

Norfolk. From Noel Coward's *Private Lives*.

4

London. From William Cobbett's *Rural Rides* (a wen is a wart, a lump, an excrescence).

5

Paris. From Ernest Hemingway, *A Moveable Feast*.

6

Blackburn, Lancashire. From the song *A Day in the Life* by Lennon and McCartney.

7

Venice. Truman Capote. (Robert Benchley once cabled Harold Ross of *The New Yorker* from Venice: 'STREETS FULL OF WATER. PLEASE ADVISE.')

8

Oxford. From Matthew Arnold, *Essays in Criticism*.

9

Paris. Thomas Appleton.

10

America. Oscar Wilde.

Washington Post

SPECIAL EDITION

EXPLETIVE DELETED

The Wit and Wisdom of Richard M Nixon.

You won't have
Nixon to kick
around any more.

*To reporters,
on failing to become
Governor
of California, 1962.*

This certainly has
to be the most
historic telephone
call ever made.

*To the first men on
the moon, 1969.*

This is the greatest
week in the history
of the world
since the Creation.

*When they came
back from the moon.*

I don't give a shit
about the lira.

23 June, 1972.

I am not a crook.

17 November, 1973.

Ars Longa, Vita Sackville-West

Music and musicians

Wagner is the Puccini of music.

> *Beachcomber (J. B. Morton).*

I liked your opera. I think I will set it to music.

> *Beethoven to fellow composer.*

The greatest composers since Beethoven.

> *Richard Buckle on the Beatles.*

There are only two things requisite so far as the
public is concerned for a good performance. That is
for the orchestra to begin together and end together.
In between it doesn't matter much.

> *Sir Thomas Beecham.*

I could eat alphabet soup and *shit* better lyrics.

> *Johnny Mercer on a British Musical.*

Actors and acting

She ran the whole gamut of emotions from A to B.

> *Dorothy Parker on Katherine
> Hepburn (adding that another actress
> kept upstage of Miss H. 'lest she
> catch acting from her'.)*

It made me feel that Albert had married beneath his
station.

> *Noel Coward on an inadequate
> portrayal of Queen Victoria.*

Ears too big.

> *Verdict on Clark Gable's first screen
> test.*

Let my people go!

Lenny Bruce half-way through
Exodus, *the lengthy film about the founding of modern Israel.*

Art and artists

The portrait is a very remarkable example of modern art. It certainly combines force with candour.

Churchill, on being presented with his portrait painted by Graham Sutherland. Lady Churchill's criticism took a more practical form. She ordered it to be destroyed.

My god, they've shot the wrong person!

James Pryde, at the unveiling of a statue to Nurse Edith Cavell.

Critics and criticism

The characteristic sound of the English Sunday: Harold Hobson barking up the wrong tree.

Penelope Gilliatt.

Asking a working writer what he thinks about critics is like asking a lamp-post how it feels about dogs.

Christopher Hampton.

It seems to me that giving Clive Barnes his CBE for services to the theatre is like giving Goering the DFC for services to the RAF.

Alan Bennett.

Self-criticism?

The purpose of satire it has been rightly said is to strip off the veneer of comforting illusion and cosy half-truth. And our job, as I see it, is to put it back again.

Michael Flanders of Flanders and Swann.

Nothing happens, nobody comes, nobody goes, it's awful.

> *Samuel Beckett*, Waiting for Godot.

It is as good as having a Government licence to print money.

> *Lord Thomson of Fleet in the early days of commercial TV.*

All my shows are great. Some of them are bad. But they are all great.

> *Lew Grade.*

I cried all the way to the bank.

> *Liberace on his reaction to adverse criticism. Now he says he owns the bank.*

<u>Thought for the Day</u>

Would you rather be in the light with the wise virgins
– or in the dark with the foolish ones?

Kinquering Congs Their Titles Take – 3

Where are the titles of these films taken from – apart,
that is, from any books they may be based on?

The answers are over the page.

1

Kind Hearts and Coronets.

2

Days of Wine and Roses.

3

Gone with the Wind.

4

Tender is the Night.

5

Mean Streets.

6

Splendour in the Grass.

7

Paths of Glory.

8

Go West, Young Man.

9

Twilight's Last Gleaming.

10

None but the Brave.

11

Ill Met by Moonlight.

12

Lilies of the Field.

13

Behold a Pale Horse.

14

Deadlier than the Male.

Answers

Kinquering Congs Their Titles Take – 3

1 'Howe'er it be, it seems to me, / 'Tis only noble to be good. / Kind hearts are more than coronets, / And simple faith than Norman blood' – Tennyson, *Lady Clara Vere de Vere*.

2 'They are not long, the days of wine and roses' – Ernest Dowson, *Vitae Summa Brevis*.

3 'I have forgot much, Cynara. Gone with the wind' – Ernest Dowson, *Non Sum Qualis Eram*.

4 'Already with thee! Tender is the night' – Keats, *Ode to a Nightingale*.

5 'Down these mean streets a man must go who is not himself mean; who is neither tarnished nor afraid' – Raymond Chandler, *The Simple Art of Murder*.

6 'Though nothing can bring back the hour / Of splendour in the grass, of glory in the flower' – Wordsworth, *Ode (Intimations of Immortality)*.

7 'The boast of heraldry, the pomp of power, / And all that beauty, all that wealth e'er gave, / Awaits alike th'inevitable hour, / The paths of glory lead but to the grave' – Gray, *Elegy Written in a Country Churchyard*.

8 'Go west, young man, and grow up with the country' – Horace Greeley, based on J. B. L. Soule.

9 'Oh, say, can you see by the dawn's early light, / What so proudly we hailed at the twilight's last gleaming?' – Francis Scott Key, *The Star-Spangled Banner*.

10 'None but the brave deserves the fair' – Dryden, *Alexander's Feast*.

11 'Ill met by moonlight, proud Titania' – Shakespeare, *A Midsummer Night's Dream*, II.i.

12 'Consider the lilies of the field, how they grow' – St Matthew vi.28 (the Sermon on the Mount).

13 'And I looked, and behold a pale horse: and his name that sat on him was death' – Revelation vi.8.

14 'For the female of the species is more deadly than the male' – Kipling, *The Female of the Species*. This is one of a remarkable number of phrases that Kipling gave to the language: 'white man's burden', 'somewhere East of Suez', 'he travels fastest who travels alone', 'the widow at Windsor', 'flannelled fools', and 'East is East and West is West, and never the twain shall meet'.

None but the brave

Ill met by moonlight

Splendour in the grass

The paths of glory

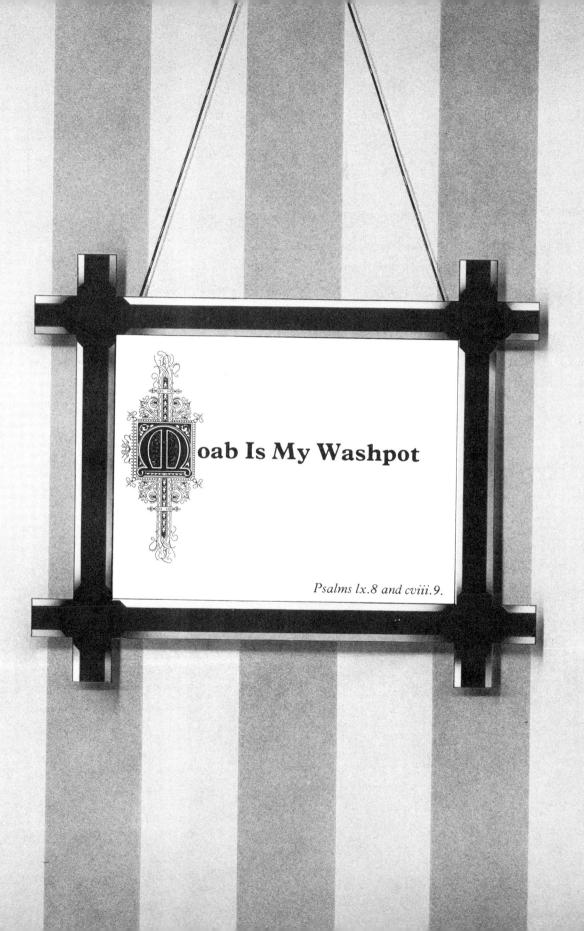

Seldom is a quotation given more prominence than when it is the text for a sermon. It is perhaps spoken twice at the beginning and once at the end. Whether what is said in between has any connection with it is, of course, quite another matter – memorably demonstrated by Alan Bennett in his *Beyond the Fringe* sermon. He took as his text a scrambled version of Genesis xxvii.ll:

And he said, my brother Esau is an hairy man, but I
am a smooth man.

Listen out for sermons based on the following:

Moab is my washpot; over Edom will I cast out my
shoe.

Psalms lx.8 and cviii.9.

My beloved put his hand in by the hole of the door,
and my bowels were moved for him.

Solomon v.4.

And it came to pass that he fell off the seat back-
ward: for he was an old man, and heavy.

1 Samuel iv.18.

Go up, thou bald head; go up, thou bald head.

2 Kings ii.23.

Isn't God a shit!

*Randolph Churchill, while reading
the Bible from cover to cover in
response to Evelyn Waugh's bet of
£10 that he could not do so.*

I have spent a lot of time searching through the
Bible for loopholes.

W. C. Fields.

Better Left Unsaid

Although he was not a politician, Lieutenant-Commander Tommy Woodrooffe was one of the first men to appreciate broadcasting's enormous potential for helping you put your foot in it – for allowing you to say things you would later regret and which would haunt you to the end of your days.

Describing the illumination of the Fleet at the Spithead Review in 1937, he said:

> At the present moment, the whole fleet is lit up . . . when I say 'lit up', I mean lit up by fairy lamps.

Naturally, everyone concluded that Woodrooffe was himself 'lit up' as the result of too much hospitality from his former shipmates on board H.M.S. *Nelson*. But he denied this. 'I was so overcome by the occasion that I literally burst into tears . . . I had a kind of nervous black-out. I had been working too hard and my mind just went blank.'

During the Three-Day Week in 1974, Energy Minister Patrick Jenkin had an energy-saving idea. He was photographed using his electric razor by candlelight, and added:

> People can clean their teeth in the dark.

In March 1966, John Lennon of the Beatles gave a newspaper interview in which he said:

> Christianity will go. It will vanish and shrink. I needn't argue about that. I'm right and I'll be proved right. We're more popular than Jesus now.

The remark lay dormant for several months but when the Beatles paid a visit to the United States it was reprinted and caused an outcry. Lennon subsequently had to withdraw it.

In 1961, before becoming Prime Minister, Harold Wilson said:

> I myself have always deprecated . . . appeals to the Dunkirk spirit as an answer to our problem.

But – lo! – within months of taking office in 1964 he was saying:

> I believe that the spirit of Dunkirk will once again carry us through to success.

In July 1957, Harold Macmillan said:

> You've never had it so good.

He was echoing a US presidential election slogan from 1952 and although the context makes it clear that the remark was intended as a warning and not as a complacent boast ('What is beginning to worry some of us is "Is it too good to be true?" Or perhaps I should say "Is it too good to last?"') the phrase dogged him thereafter.

Ian Smith, March 1976:

> I don't believe in black majority rule ever in Rhodesia . . . not in a thousand years.

Harold Wilson, January 1966:

> The cumulative effects of the economic and financial sanctions [against Rhodesia] might well bring the rebellion to an end within a matter of weeks rather than months.

Edward Heath acquired two hostages to fortune within the space of a month before becoming Prime Minister in June 1970. On 5 May he addressed the Franco-British Chamber of Commerce in Paris. Looking ahead to the enlargement of the EEC he said that this would not be in the interests of the Community:

> Except with the *full-hearted consent of the Parliament and people* of the new member countries.

This statement (written, incidentally, by Douglas Hurd, a Heath aide) was seized upon later by those seeking a referendum on EEC entry.

The phrase which haunted Edward Heath most, however, was one that never even passed his lips. A press release made available at a Tory press conference contained the promise that a Conservative Government would:

> *At a stroke* reduce the rise in prices, increase productivity and reduce unemployment.

President Gerald R. Ford was noted more for physical than verbal ineptitude – but only by a narrow margin. In December 1975 he proposed a toast to Anwar Sadat with the words:

The President of Israel!

He probably scotched his chances of re-election in 1976 during one of the TV debates with his challenger, Jimmy Carter, by declaring that:

There is no Soviet domination of Eastern Europe.

In the same campaign, Carter gave an interview to *Playboy* magazine and said:

I've looked on a lot of women with lust. I've committed adultery in my heart many times. God recognises I will do this and forgives me.

The American electorate, perceiving a useful working relationship with the Almighty, let Carter off.

Walter Annenberg, US Ambassador to the Court of St James went to present his credentials to the Queen in 1969. Unfortunately for him a TV crew was hovering at his elbow making the film *Royal Family*. So millions were able to hear the peculiarly orotund remarks he thought appropriate for the occasion. When asked by the Queen about his official residence he admitted to:

> Some discomfiture as a result of a need for elements of refurbishing.

In his TV address after the devaluation of the pound in November 1967, Harold Wilson said:

> From now on the pound abroad is worth 14% or so less in terms of other currencies. That doesn't mean of course that *the pound* here in Britain, *in your pocket* or purse or in your bank, has been devalued. What it does mean is that we shall now be able to sell more goods abroad on a competitive basis.

A year later Edward Heath asked Wilson whether on reconsideration he would still have made the remark:

> As to the accuracy of what I said, the answer is, Yes. But recalling the warning of Rudyard Kipling,
>
> > *If you can bear to hear the truth you've spoken,*
> > *Twisted by knaves to make a trap for fools . . .*
>
> I might have had second thoughts.

Like The Curate's Egg – 2

More scrambled quotations for you to go to work on.
The answers are on page 84

1

That first careless rupture.

2

Gone to that country from whose Bourne no Hollingsworth
returns.

3

They are rolling up the maps all over Europe. We shall not
see them lit again in our lifetime.

4

All women dress like their mothers, that is their tragedy. No
man ever does. That is his.

5

An honour is not without profit, except in your own country.

6

A rose by any other name as sweet would smell –
a rhododendron, by any other name, would be much
easier to spell.

7

Absinthe makes the heart grow fonder.

8

The money that men make lives after them.

9

If you have ears, prepare to shed them now.

10

It is a far, far butter thing.

11

When I hear the word 'vulture', I reach for my revolver.

12

At my back I often hear / Time's winged chariot changing
gear.

13

A bachelor never quite gets over the idea that he is a thing of
beauty and a boy forever.

Answers
Like The Curate's Egg – 2

1 'That's the wise thrush; he sings each song twice over, / Lest you should think he never could recapture / The first fine careless rapture!' – Browning, *Home-thoughts, from abroad*.

2 'Death / The undiscover'd country from whose bourn / No traveller returns' – Shakespeare, *Hamlet*, III.i. (scrambled by Beachcomber).

3 'The lamps are going out all over Europe; we shall not see them lit again in our lifetime' – Sir Edward Grey, 1914, and 'Roll up that map [of Europe]; it will not be wanted these few years' – William Pitt the Younger after the battle of Austerlitz (scrambled by Alan Bennett).

4 All women become like their mothers, that is their tragedy. No man ever does. That is his' – Wilde, *The Importance of Being Earnest* (scrambled by Alan Bennett).

5 'A prophet is not without honour, save in his own country and in his own house' – St Matthew xiii.57 (scrambled by Michael Flanders).

6 'What's in a name? That which we call a rose / By any other name would smell as sweet' – Shakespeare, *Romeo and Juliet*, II.ii.

7 'Absence makes the heart grow fonder' – the proverb (scrambled by Oscar Wilde).

8 'The evil that men do lives after them. / The good is oft interred with their bones' – Shakespeare, *Julius Caesar*, III.ii. (scrambled by Samuel Butler – before death duties).

9 'If you have tears, prepare to shed them now' – Shakespeare, *Julius Caesar*, III.ii.

10 'It is a far, far better thing that I do, than I have ever done; it is a far, far better rest that I go to, than I have ever known' – Charles Dickens, *A Tale of Two Cities* (scrambled as a slogan by Dorothy L. Sayers in *Murder Must Advertise*).

11 'When I hear the word "culture", I reach for my revolver' – words usually attributed to Goering.

12 'But at my back I always hear / Time's wingèd chariot hurrying near' – Marvell, *To His Coy Mistress* (scrambled by Eric Linklater).

13 'A thing of beauty is a joy for ever' – Keats *Endymion* (scrambled by Helen Rowland).

**Famous
Last
Words**

The story is told of the relative of a dying man who – eager
to record his last words for posterity – bent her ear down to
catch his latest breath only to hear him say, 'Boo!'
Last words are not something you can have a second
stab at and only a few manage to go out with a memorable or
appropriate saying on their lips:

Get my swan costume ready.

> *Anna Pavlova, affirming that even*
> in extremis *the show must go on.*

I shall hear in heaven.

> *Beethoven, optimistic on two counts.*

Mozart!

> *Mahler. For technical reasons*
> *Mozart was unable to reciprocate.*

The sun is God.

> *J. M. W. Turner.*

I've had eighteen straight whiskies. I think it is a
record.

> *Dylan Thomas* (he had probably
> drunk only four or five).

Could have done better

I am Heinrich Himmler.

> *Heinrich Himmler* (no really).

I want my lunch.

> *J. Paul Getty.*

Have you brought the cheque-book, Alfred?

> *Samuel Butler.*

Write your own epitaph

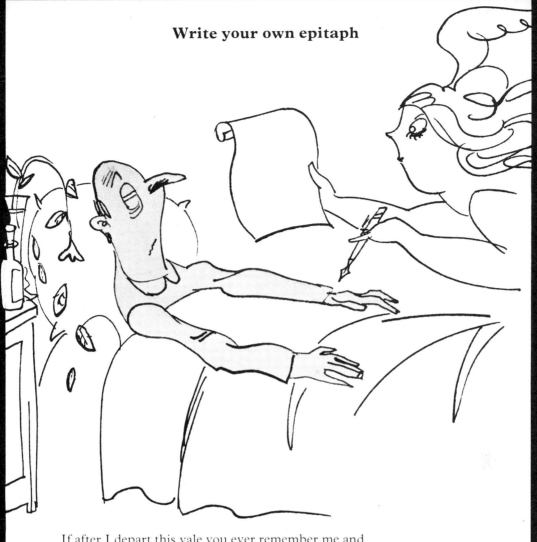

If after I depart this vale you ever remember me and have thought to please my ghost, forgive some sinner and wink your eye at some homely girl.

H. L. Mencken.

He never used a sentence where a paragraph would do.

Huw Wheldon.

On the whole I'd rather be in Philadelphia.

W. C. Fields.

Trying too hard

My exit is the result of too many entrées.

> *Richard Monckton-Milnes.*

Ah well, I suppose I shall have to die beyond my means.

> *Oscar Wilde, on being told the cost of an operation.*

False alarms

You should have known that it was not easy for me to die. But, tell me, were my obituaries good?

> *President Makarios, 1974.*

I'm super-jew!

> *Lenny Bruce, leaping from a window but only sustaining a broken leg.*

Drawing peacefully to a close

No, it is better not. She would only ask me to take a message to Albert.

Disraeli, when it was suggested to him that he might like a visit from Queen Victoria.

What's the question?

Gertrude Stein, when asked by bosom-pal Alice B. Toklas, 'What's the answer, what's the answer?'

Alternative versions

1 I have been an unconscionable time dying and I hope you will excuse it.
2 Don't let poor Nellie starve.

Charles II has both these sets of dying words attributed to him.

1 How is the Empire?
2 Gentlemen. I am sorry for keeping you waiting like this. I am unable to concentrate.
3 Bugger Bognor.

George V runs to three sets – the last in response to a courtier who suggested that the King would soon be well enough to visit his favourite seaside resort.

Epitaphs

A man of much courage and superb equipment.

On Brigham Young, the Mormon leader, who died leaving seventeen or more wives.

Ars longa, vita brevis.

On Thomas Longbottom.

Under this sod lies another one.

On Anon.

Appendix*

*Please cut out.

Princess Anne (Mrs Mark Phillips) (1950–   )
One flew over the cuckoo's nest. *Attrib.*

Mark Antony (*c.* 82–30 B.C.)
The biggest asp-disaster in the world. *On the death of Cleopatra*

John Logie Baird (1888–1946)
I think I will just turn over and see if there is anything on the other
side. *Last words*

Mrs Beeton (1836–65)
I think I am just about done now. *Last words*

Alexander Graham Bell (1847–1922)
Dead, dead . . . and never called me mother. *Last words*

Charles Dickens (1812–1870)
Compliments to the chef, but I think the sauce was a little brutal this
evening. *Oliver Twist*, chap. 2

General Franco (1892–1975)
Yes, we have no *mañanas*. *Last words*

W. G. Grace (1848–1915)
Congratulations on your overnight stand. *To Casanova*

Ernest Hemingway (1898–1961)
A farewell to arms. *Of the Venus de Milo*

Herod Antipas (?–*c.* A.D. 40)
Sorry, dear, brains are off. *To Salome when she asked for John the
Baptist's head on a platter*

Lenin (Vladimir Ilyich Ulyanov) (1870–1924)
I was born under a squandering Tsar. *Attrib.*

Napoleon I (Napoleon Bonaparte) (1769–1821)
C'est magnifique, mais ce n'est pas la gare. *On arriving at Euston
instead of Waterloo*

William Pitt (1759–1806)
Oh god! I think I have just eaten one of Bellamy's veal pies. *Last
words*

Sir Walter Ralegh (*c.* 1552–1618)
Be of good comfort, Master Ridley. We shall this day light such a
candle by God's grace as I trust shall never be put out. *On introducing
tobacco to England*

Richard III (1452–85)
A hearse, a hearse . . . my kingdom for a hearse! *Last words*

Marquis De Sade (1740–1814)
This is going to hurt me more than it hurts you. *Last words*

Madame Tussaud (1761–1850)
Once I was waxing—now I am waning. *Last words*

Henri De Toulouse-Lautrec (1864-1901)
Come down and see me some time.

Queen Victoria (1819–1901)
The Empire's decision is funereal. *Last words*

INDEX

Envoi

Go! And never darken my towels again!

Groucho Marx, Duck Soup.